Biology

by Martha Schmitt

TABLE OF CONTENTS

PAGE	TITLE	CONCEPTS
1	Identifying the Design of an Experiment	Variables in an Experiment
2	What Plants and Animals Need to Live	Requirements for Life
3	How Plant and Animal Cells Differ	Characteristics of Plant and Animal Cells
4	The Cell's Control Center	Chromosomes, DNA, and Genes
5	How Body Cells Divide	Mitosis
6	How Sex Cells Form	Meiosis
7	Parts of a Fern	Structure of Nonflowering Plants
8	Parts of a Flowering Plant	Structure of Flowering Plants
9	How Plants and Animals Reproduce	Asexual and Sexual Reproduction
10	Inheriting Blood Types	Principles of Inheritance
11	How Plants Make Food	Photosynthesis
12	How Plants and Animals Use Food	Respiration
13	Classifying Living Things	The Five Kingdoms of Living Things
14	The Roles of Simple Organisms	Microorganisms
15	Crossword Puzzle on Plants	Classification of Plants into Divisions
16	Classifying Animals by Phylum	Classification of Animals into Phyla
17	Classifying Backboned Animals	Vertebrate Classes
18	Where Plants and Animals Live	Classifying Plants and Animals by Biomes
19	Primary Succession on a Beach Dune	Ecological Succession
20	People and the Environment	Effects of Human Population Growth
21	The Breath of Life	Human Respiratory System
22	The Heart Chart	Human Circulatory System
23	Reflex Actions	Human Nervous System
24	How You Digest Food	Human Digestive System
25	Planning Nutritious Meals	Human Nutrition
26	Crossword Puzzle of the Human Skeleton	Human Skeletal System
27	The Three Kinds of Muscles	Human Muscular System
28	How the Immune System Works	Human Immune System

Teacher's Guide

Biology is designed to supplement and enrich the science program for grades six, seven, eight, and nine. The pages feature a variety of activities that require students to think about and apply what they have learned about biology. These activities include labeling, interpreting, and drawing diagrams; writing captions for diagrams; completing charts; and interpreting charts and graphs.

Answers

Page 1
1. the dish without any salt solution
2. the amount of bacterial growth
3. the concentration of the salt solution
4. the unexposed group of plants
5. the condition and growth of the plants
6. the various pollutants placed on the plants

Page 2

Plants	Both plants and animals
Carbon dioxide	Nutrients
Sunlight	Oxygen
	Suitable temperature
	Water

Page 3
1. Cell wall
2. Chloroplast
3. Vacuole
4. Cell membrane
5. Nucleus
6. Cytoplasm
7. Plant cells have cell walls and chloroplasts, which animal cells lack. The vacuoles in plant cells are much larger than the vacuoles in animal cells.
8. Cell wall: holds the cell together by counteracting the pressure created by the water in the vacuole
   Cell membrane: holds the cell together and regulates the movement of substances into and out of the cell
   Chloroplasts: carry on photosynthesis
   Cytoplasm: contains many structures that carry out the activities of the cell
   Nucleus: directs the activities of the cell
   Vacuole: serves as a reservoir for water and other substances the cell uses as well as for wastes

Page 4
1. True   2. False   3. True   4. True
5. True   6. False   7. False 8. True
9. False 10. True 11. True 12. False

Page 5
1.
2.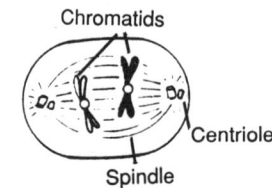
3.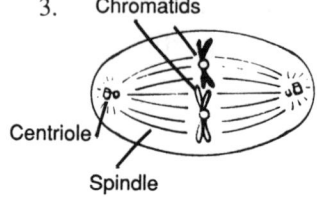
4.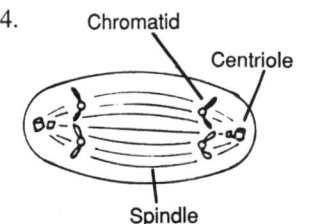
5.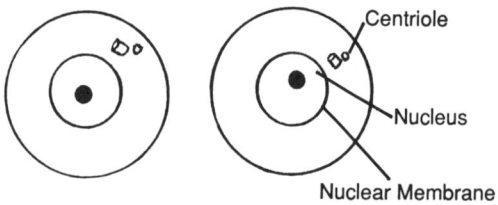

Page 6
1. The chromosomes and the centrioles duplicate. The centrioles start moving to opposite sides of the cell. Similar chromosomes line up together.
2. Double pairs of chromosomes go to the middle of the spindle and separate, moving to opposite sides of the cell.
3. The cell splits in two, in the first division of meiosis.
4. The chromatids separate, and the cell starts to divide again.
5. The second division is completed, forming four cells with one chromosome of each pair.

Page 7
1. spore   2. frond
3. rhizome   4. rhizoid
5. Rhizomes are horizontal stems that grow underground. Roots and leaves grow from the rhizomes. Like other stems, rhizomes transport water and nutrients between the leaves and roots.
6. Fronds carry out photosynthesis and bear spores.
7. Rhizoids act like roots; they absorb water and minerals from the soil.
8. Spores grow on the fronds of the fern. A spore falls to the ground and grows into a gametophyte, a plant that has male and female sex cells and produces a fertilized egg. The fertilized egg grows into a sporophyte.

Page 8
1. Flower   2. Leaf   3. Stem
4. Root   5. Stigma   6. Style
7. Ovary   8. Carpel   9. Anther
10. Filament   11. Stamen
12. Flower: reproduction
    Leaf: produces food and gives off oxygen and water
    Stem: transports water and nutrients throughout the plant; supports the leaves and flowers
    Root: absorbs water and minerals from the soil; anchors the plant
13. Pollen from the anther reaches the stigma. A pollen tube grows to the ovary, and sperm cells travel down. A sperm cell fertilizes an egg cell; another sperm cell fuses with the polar nuclei. From this double fertilization, a seed develops. When the seed falls to the ground, a new plant grows.

Page 9
1. D   2. H   3. B   4. C
5. I   6. E   7. G   8. F
9. J   10. A

Page 10
2. Possible Combinations in Offspring: AB, AO, AB, AO
   Possible blood types of offspring: AB or A
3. Possible Combinations in Offspring: AB, AO, BO, OO
   Possible blood types of offspring: AB, A, B, or O
4. Possible Combinations in Offspring: AA, AB, AB, BB
   Possible blood types of offspring: A, AB, or B

Page 11
Part A
1. light energy   2. chloroplasts
3. leaves   4. chlorophyll
5. chemical energy   6. carbon dioxide
7. water   8. hydrogen
9. oxygen   10. glucose

Part B
Students' diagrams may vary. The following diagram is an example.

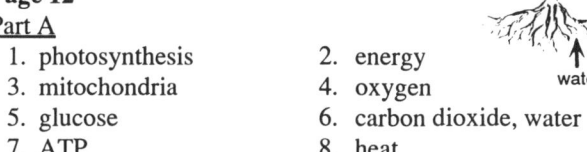

Page 12
Part A
1. photosynthesis   2. energy
3. mitochondria   4. oxygen
5. glucose   6. carbon dioxide, water
7. ATP   8. heat

Part B
ATP, water, carbon dioxide, heat

Page 13
Monera: Bacteria, Blue-green algae, Spirochete
Protists: Amoeba, Ciliate, Diatom
Fungi: Bread mold, Mushroom, Yeast
Plants: Fern, Moss, Lilac bush, Oak tree
Animals: Earthworm, Horse, Jellyfish, Spider

Page 14
1. True   2. True   3. False   4. False
5. True   6. True   7. False   8. True
9. True   10. True   11. False 12. False
13. True   14. True   15. False

Page 15
Across
1. Liverworts, hornworts, and mosses, which do not have true leaves, stems, or roots
4. Gingko, a deciduous tree with fan-shaped leaves
6. Conifers, which are mostly evergreen trees and shrubs that produce woody cones
8. Horsetails, which have ribbed, jointed stems

Down
2. Whisk ferns, which have highly branched stems
3. Club mosses and quillworts, which produce a leaf with one central vein
4. A group of plants that produce seeds enveloped in modified leaves
5. Flowering plants
6. Cycads, which are palmlike plants
7. Ferns, which have feathery leaves called fronds

Page 16
The specific animals that students list in each phylum may vary.
1. have a notochord at some time in their lives; gorilla, eagle, lizard, frog, fish
2. spiny-skinned animals; starfish, sea urchin, sea lily
3. soft-bodied animals; snail, octopus, clam, slug
4. have chelicerae (pincers or fangs) and four pairs of walking legs; spider, scorpion, horseshoe crab
5. have mandibles and segmented bodies; butterfly, bee, fly
6. have legs on their thorax and abdomen; crab, lobster, crayfish
7. segmented worms; earthworm, ragworm, leech
8. worms with soft, thin, flattened bodies; flatworm, tapeworm, fluke
9. have cnidocysts or stinging cells; sea anemone, jellyfish, coral
10. feed by circulating water through pores and canals; sponges

Page 17
1. Reptile   2. Amphibian   3. Bird
4. Mammal   5. Mammal   6. Reptile
7. Bird   8. Reptile   9. Mammal
10. Fish   11. Bird   12. Mammal
13. Amphibian 14. Mammal   15. Reptile
16. Bird   17. Mammal   18. Reptile
19. Fish   20. Bird

Page 18
The types of plants and animals students list may vary. The following are some examples.
1. cacti and other succulents, bushes, shrubs; burrowing mammals, lizards, snakes
2. tall and short grasses; bison, antelope, prairie dog
3. grass and widely spaced deciduous trees; zebra, giraffe, lion
4. coniferous trees, such as spruce, hemlock, and fir; elk, moose, bear, wolves
5. broadleaf deciduous trees, perennial herbs; deer, raccoon, opossum
6. broadleaf evergreen trees, vines, ferns; monkeys, snakes, jaguar, parrots
7. low shrubs, lichens; caribou, lemmings, musk-oxen, wolves

Page 19
1. It refers to the process by which plant and animal communities succeed one another over a long period of time until they reach a stable, reproducing community.
2. the beachgrass
3. the broadleaf trees
4. The animal community would change along with the changing plant cover.
5. It acquires more organic matter from dying plants and animals and so becomes richer in nutrients.

Page 20
1. 124 years
2. 49 years
3. 11 years
4. 112 years
5. The rate of population growth is increasing dramatically.
6. Students' answers will vary. Students should note that the increase in the human population would result in an increase in the use of natural resources and an increase in the amount of waste produced. Wildlife habitats would be lost as people sought land for living space and for growing crops and manufacturing goods. A decrease in the number of wild animal and plant species might be expected, as well as a decrease in the number of undisturbed ecosystems in general.

Page 21
1. trachea
2. bronchus
3. bronchiole
4. oxygen
5. carbon dioxide
6. lungs
7. capillaries
8. cells
9. energy
10. exhaled

Page 22
1. Carry blood from throughout the body to the right atrium and ventricle
2. Pump blood to the lungs, where the blood picks up oxygen
3. Open and close to regulate blood flow through the chambers of the heart
4. Pump oxygenated blood throughout the body
5. Carry oxygenated blood to all parts of the body
6. Connect the arteries and the veins and allow the exchange of oxygen and carbon dioxide
7. Carries blood from the left ventricle
8. Transports blood from the right ventricle to the lungs
9. Supply blood to the heart muscle itself
10. Transport blood from the lungs to the left atrium
11. Carries blood from the head and arms to the right atrium
12. Carries blood from the trunk and legs to the right atrium

Page 23
1. A person receives a tap below the kneecap, which hits the tendon there.
2. The tap on the tendon stretches the muscle.
3. The stretched muscle stimulates neurons called receptors.
4. The receptors produce an impulse.
5. The impulse travels along the axon of a sensory neuron to the spinal cord.
6. The impulse passes through a synapse to a motor neuron.
7. The motor neuron generates a second impulse.
8. The second impulse is transmitted along the axon of the motor neuron.
9. The second impulse reaches the muscle that was stretched, causing the muscle to contract.
10. The leg jerks.
11. The whole process is complete and took only a fraction of a second.

Page 24
1. Teeth: Chop and grind food
2. Salivary glands: Moisten the food and start to break down starches
3. Esophagus: Moves the food to the stomach
4. Stomach: Acids and enzymes start to break down proteins
5. Small intestine, pancreas, liver: Break down carbohydrates, fats, and proteins. The pancreas secretes enzymes and the liver secretes bile to break down food. The broken down food is absorbed by blood and lymph vessels in the small intestine and transported throughout the body.
6. Large intestine: Primarily compacts solid wastes, but also absorbs water and some chemicals
7. Rectum: Holds solid wastes until they are eliminated from the body

Page 25
Students' meal plans will vary, but they should meet the guidelines provided.

Page 26

Page 27
Part A
1. Skeletal
2. Smooth
3. Skeletal
4. Cardiac
5. Smooth
6. Skeletal
7. Cardiac
8. Smooth
9. Smooth
10. Skeletal

Part B
11. False
12. True
13. False
14. True
15. True

Page 28
1. white blood cells
2. antigens
3. phagocytes, lymphocytes
4. engulfs
5. T cells, B cells
6. macrophages
7. virus
8. bacteria
9. antibodies
10. long-term protection

Name _____   Variables in an Experiment

Identifying the Design of an Experiment

Experiments involve control and experimental groups. A control is the subject that does not receive the experimental treatment. The experimental group is tested in some way.

An experimental group has two variables: independent variables and dependent variables. The independent variable is the material one works with during an experiment. The dependent variable is what is being measured or observed.

Read the following descriptions of biology experiments. For each one, identify the control, the dependent variable, and the independent variable.

A. A biology class wants to investigate what concentration of a salt solution is most effective in preventing the growth of bacteria. Students prepare five dishes of agar (a gelatin-like substance used to cultivate living material). They spread solutions of different salt concentrations on four dishes, leaving one dish untouched. Then they introduce bacteria on all the dishes and observe the dishes for the amount of bacterial growth.

1. Control _____
2. Dependent variable _____
3. Independent variable _____

B. An ecologist wants to investigate the effects of pollution on soybean plants. The scientist grows five groups of plants and exposes four groups to various pollutants. The fifth group is not exposed to any pollutant. The ecologist observes the condition and growth of all the groups of plants over a period of time.

4. Control _____
5. Dependent variable _____
6. Independent variable _____

Extension Activity: Write a description of a biology experiment you would like to conduct. Identify the control, the dependent variable, and the independent variable in your experiment.

Name _____   Requirements for Life

What Plants and Animals Need to Live

What are the essential things that most plants and animals need to survive? Use the words in the box to complete the Venn diagram. Write the things that both plants and animals need in the overlapping area. Write the things that plants alone need on the left side. Write the things that animals alone need on the right side.

Carbon dioxide	Oxygen	Sunlight
Nutrients	Suitable temperature	Water

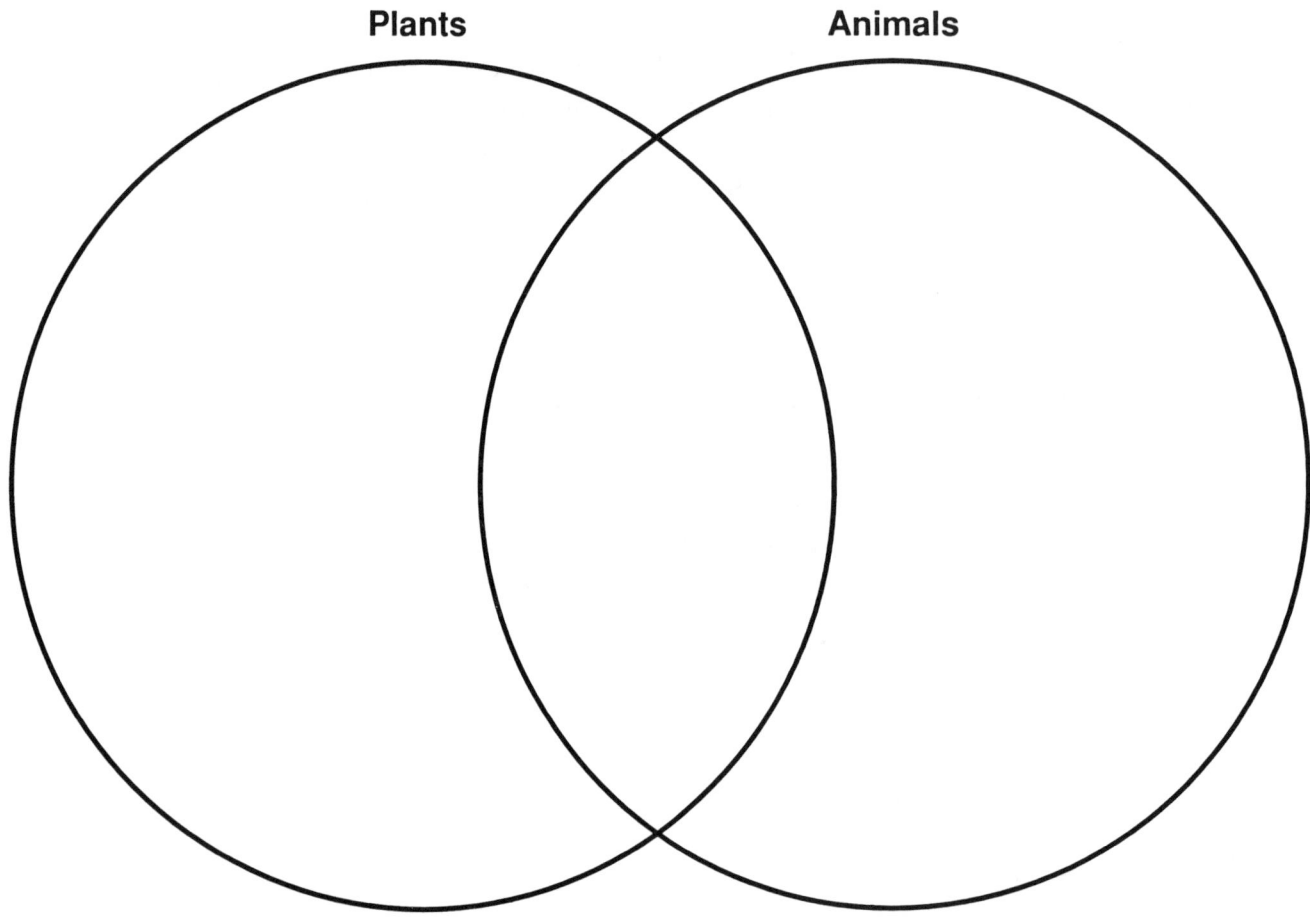

Extension Activity: Design and carry out an experiment with plants to investigate their requirements for life. Vary the amount of water, sunlight, temperature, and/or the soil conditions.

Name _____   Characteristics of Plant and Animal Cells

How Plant and Animal Cells Differ

The diagrams below show some basic parts of typical plant and animal cells. Label the diagrams, using the words in the box. Then answer the questions.

Plant Cell   **Animal Cell**

| Cell wall |
| Cell membrane |
| Chloroplast |
| Cytoplasm |
| Nucleus |
| Vacuole |

1. _____
2. _____
3. _____
4. _____
5. _____
6. _____

7. How do plant cells differ from animal cells? _____
   _____

8. What is the function of each of the following cell parts?
   Cell wall _____
   _____

   Cell membrane _____
   _____

   Chloroplasts _____
   _____

   Cytoplasm _____
   _____

   Nucleus _____
   _____

   Vacuoles _____
   _____

Name _____   Chromosomes, DNA, and Genes

The Cell's Control Center

The diagram and caption below summarize the relationship between a chromosome, DNA, and genes. Use the diagram and your own knowledge to decide whether each statement is true or false. Write true *or* false *before each statement.*

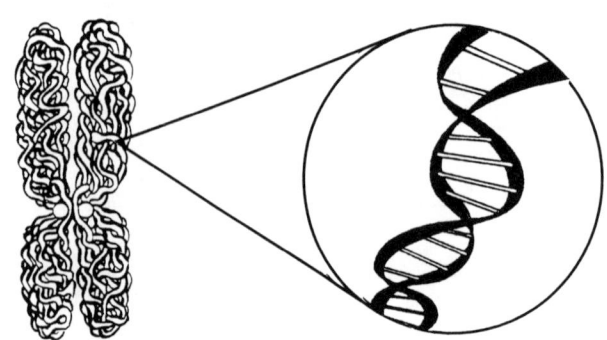

A chromosome contains protein and one long molecule of DNA, which is shaped like a twisted rope ladder. A gene is a segment of the DNA molecule. Most genes consist of thousands of rungs on the "ladder." A chromosome may have thousands of genes.

Chromosome   **Part of DNA molecule**

_____ 1. A chromosome is highly coiled.

_____ 2. Genes are larger than chromosomes.

_____ 3. Genes determine what characteristics offspring inherit.

_____ 4. A human body cell has 23 pairs of chromosomes, or 46 total.

_____ 5. DNA directs the production of proteins in a cell.

_____ 6. Chromosomes only occur in egg and sperm cells.

_____ 7. Chromosomes are located within the cytoplasm of a cell.

_____ 8. Egg and sperm cells have half as many chromosomes as other human cells do.

_____ 9. The letters *DNA* stand for *diniate*.

_____ 10. The DNA molecule has a structure that allows it to duplicate easily.

_____ 11. The shape of the DNA molecule is called a double helix.

_____ 12. Human beings have about 100 genes.

COPYRIGHT © 1993 McDONALD PUBLISHING CO.   BIOLOGY

Name _____   Mitosis

How Body Cells Divide

Mitosis is the process by which all cells other than sex cells are produced. The captions below describe the four stages of mitosis as well as interphase, the stage before mitosis begins. Draw a diagram for each caption. Include the labels provided. Use reference books if you need help.

Mitosis of an Animal Cell (Two Chromosomes Shown)

Centriole Nucleus Nucleolus Chromatids	Chromatids Centriole Spindle
Interphase 1. The chromosomes duplicate and form chromatids. The centrioles also duplicate.	**Prophase** 2. The centrioles go to the opposite sides of the cell and form a spindle across it. The nuclear membrane dissolves.
Chromatids Centriole Spindle	Chromatid Centriole Spindle
Metaphase 3. The chromatids align in the middle of the spindle.	**Anaphase** 4. The chromatids separate. The members of each pair go to opposite sides of the cell.

Nucleus   Centriole   Nuclear Membrane
Telephase 5. The cell divides, producing two new identical cells. The nuclear membrane reforms.

COPYRIGHT © 1993 McDONALD PUBLISHING CO.   5   BIOLOGY

Name _____   Meiosis

How Sex Cells Form

Meiosis is the process by which sex cells are produced. The diagrams below show the steps in this process. Write captions for the diagrams, describing how meiosis occurs.

Meiosis of an Animal Cell (4 Chromosomes Shown)

1. _____   2. _____
   _____   _____
   _____   _____
   _____   _____

3. _____   4. _____
   _____   _____
   _____   _____
   _____   _____

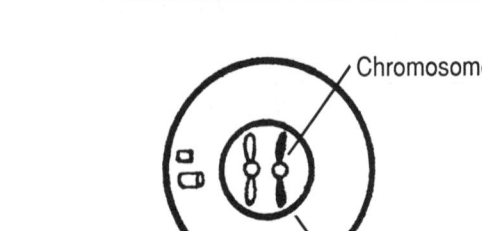 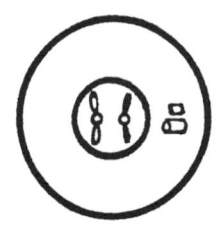  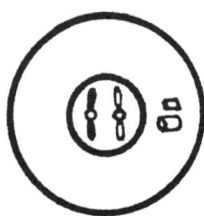

5. _____
   _____

COPYRIGHT © 1993 McDONALD PUBLISHING CO.   BIOLOGY

Name _____   Structure of Nonflowering Plants

Parts of a Fern

The diagrams at the right show the two generations of a fern plant. Label these parts on the diagrams: frond, spore, rhizome, and rhizoid. Then answer the questions below.

1. _____
2. _____
3. _____
4. _____

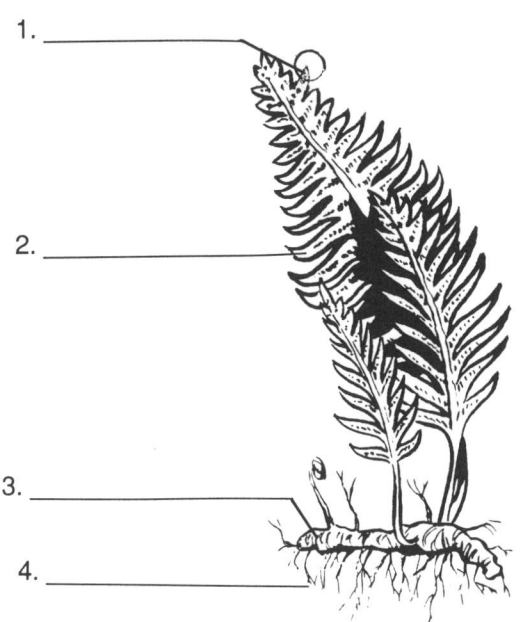 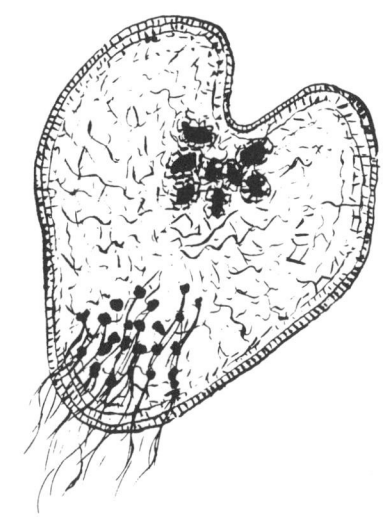

Sporophyte   **Gametophyte**

5. What is the function of rhizomes?
   _____
   _____

6. What is the function of fronds?
   _____
   _____

7. What is the function of rhizoids?
   _____
   _____

8. Describe the process by which ferns reproduce sexually.
   _____
   _____
   _____

COPYRIGHT © 1993 McDONALD PUBLISHING CO.   7   BIOLOGY

Parts of a Flowering Plant

On the two diagrams below, label the parts of a flowering plant, using the terms in the box. Then answer the questions at the bottom of the page.

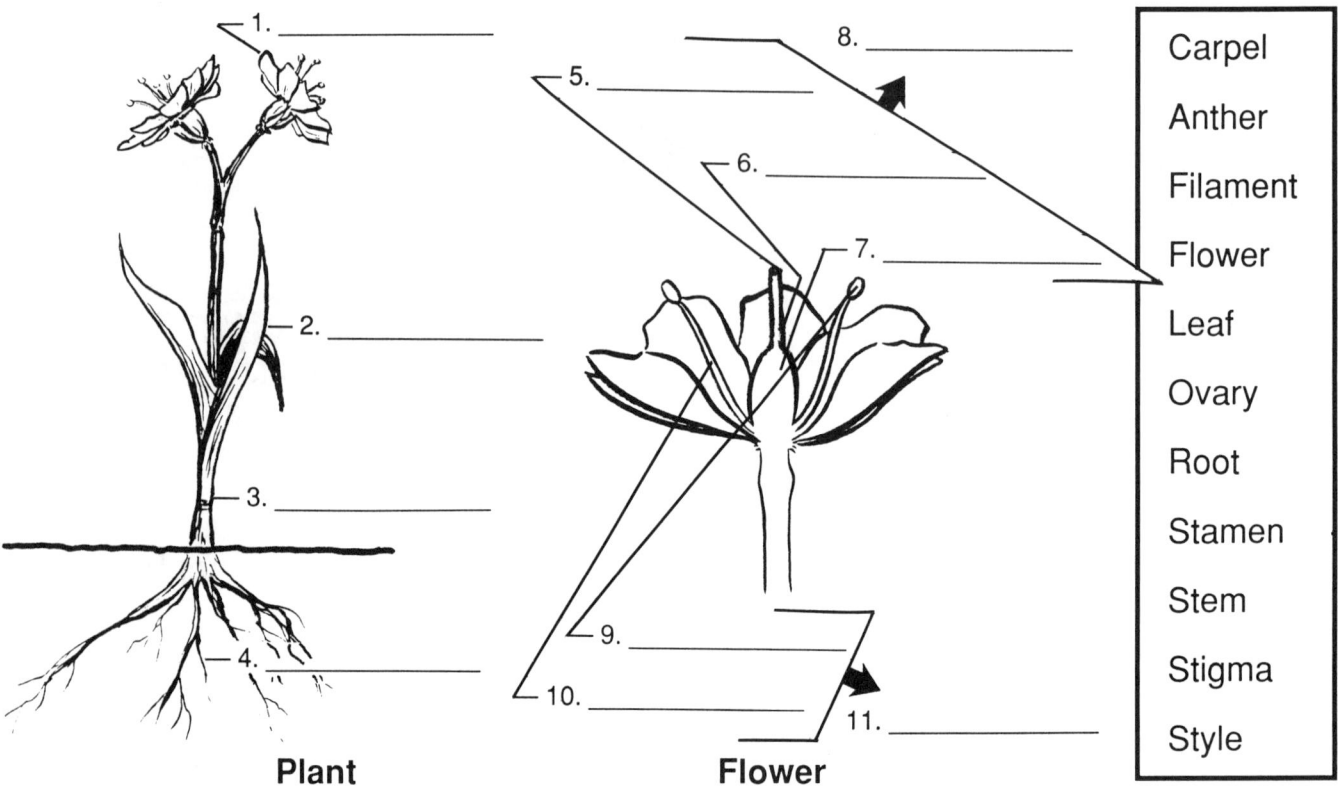

| Carpel |
| Anther |
| Filament |
| Flower |
| Leaf |
| Ovary |
| Root |
| Stamen |
| Stem |
| Stigma |
| Style |

Plant **Flower**

12. Briefly describe the function of each of these parts of a flowering plant.

   Flower _____

   Leaf _____

   Stem _____

   Root _____

13. Describe how flowering plants reproduce sexually.

   _____

   _____

   _____

   _____

Name _____   Asexual and Sexual Reproduction

How Plants and Animals Reproduce

All living things have some means of creating more of their own kind. Check your knowledge of the different ways in which plants and animals reproduce. Match each statement with the name of the process it best describes. Write the letter before each statement. Each letter will be used only once.

1. ____ An animal grows buds, which break off and form new individuals.
2. ____ A part of an animal or plant grows into a new individual.
3. ____ A new organism develops from one parent and is genetically identical to the parent.
4. ____ An organism divides into two nearly equal halves.
5. ____ Pollen from the anther of a flower is transferred to the stigma of a flower on the same plant.
6. ____ Pollen from the anther of a flower is transferred to the stigma of a flower on another plant.
7. ____ Sperm and egg unite within an animal's body.
8. ____ Sperm and egg unite outside an animal's body.
9. ____ A new organism develops from two parents and is genetically unique.
10. ____ In its life cycle, a plant regularly alternates a sexual form with an asexual form.

A. Alternation of generations
B. Asexual reproduction
C. Binary fission
D. Budding
E. Cross-pollination
F. External fertilization
G. Internal fertilization
H. Regeneration
I. Self-pollination
J. Sexual Reproduction

Extension Activity: Observe asexual reproduction in a common house plant such as a philodendron by cutting off and planting a piece of a stem with one or more nodes.

Name _____   Principles of Inheritance

Inheriting Blood Types

Use the information in the box to complete the diagrams showing possible blood types of offspring. The first one has been done for you.

> **Factors Involved in the Inheritance of Blood Type**
> - Blood type is determined by three alleles, A, B, and O, although a person has no more than two of these alleles.
> - Two of the same alleles produce that particular blood type: A, B, or O.
> - An A allele and a B allele produce AB blood type.
> - A and B are dominant over O.

1. Mother: (A) (B)   Father: (O) (O)
    Possible Combinations in Offspring: (AO) (AO) (BO) (BO)
    Possible blood types of offspring _____ A or B _____

2. Mother: (A) (A)   Father: (B) (O)
    Possible Combinations in Offspring: ( ) ( ) ( ) ( )
    Possible blood types of offspring _____

3. Mother: (A) (O)   Father: (B) (O)
    Possible Combinations in Offspring: ( ) ( ) ( ) ( )
    Possible blood types of offspring _____

4. Mother: (A) (B)   Father: (A) (B)
    Possible Combinations in Offspring: ( ) ( ) ( ) ( )
    Possible blood types of offspring _____

COPYRIGHT © 1993 McDONALD PUBLISHING CO.   BIOLOGY

Name _____   Photosynthesis

How Plants Make Food

A. The paragraphs below describe the process of photosynthesis in plants. Complete the description using the words from the box. Each word will be used only once.

| carbon dioxide | chlorophyll | glucose | leaves | oxygen |
| chemical energy | chloroplasts | hydrogen | light energy | water |

The process by which plants use (1) _____ from the sun to make food is called photosynthesis. This process occurs within dark green structures called (2) _____, which lie within a plant's (3) _____. The green pigment in the chloroplasts, called (4) _____, traps light energy. This light energy is changed into (5) _____ and stored.

A plant absorbs (6) _____ from the air and (7) _____ from the soil. The plant uses some of its stored chemical energy to split water into (8) _____ and oxygen. Most of the (9) _____ is released into the air and is used by animals. The hydrogen and carbon dioxide combine and form a simple sugar called (10) _____, which the plant may store or use for energy.

B. Draw a simple diagram to illustrate the process of photosynthesis as it is described above.

Name _____   Respiration

How Plants and Animals Use Food

A. The paragraphs below describe respiration, the process by which plants and animals release energy from glucose. Complete the description using the words from the box. Each word will be used only once.

ATP	mitochondria
carbon dioxide	oxygen
energy	photosynthesis
glucose	water
heat	

Plants make their own food through (1) _____, and animals get food when they eat plants or other animals. Plants and animals use the (2) _____ from food to carry out life processes. In a plant or animal, each cell needs energy, which it gets through respiration.

Respiration occurs within cellular structures called (3) _____. During respiration, a cell uses (4) _____ to release energy from (5) _____. Two by-products of this process are (6) _____ and _____.

Some of the energy produced during respiration gets stored in molecules called (7) _____. However, some of the energy is lost as (8) _____, which keeps an organism warm.

B. Complete the following to show what happens within a cell during respiration.

$$\text{oxygen} + \text{glucose} \xrightarrow{\text{produce}}$$

_____
_____
_____
_____

Name _____   The Five Kingdoms of Living Things

Classifying Living Things

The statements below describe the five kingdoms into which living things are divided. Use the statements to classify the list of living things. Write the name of each organism in the correct column in the chart.

Monera: Simple, one-celled organisms that lack a nucleus

Protists: Mainly one-celled organisms that contain a nucleus

Fungi: Multi-celled organisms that absorb their food from dead or living things

Plants: Mainly multi-celled organisms that make their own food through photosynthesis

Animals: Multi-celled organisms that ingest their food

Amoeba
Bacteria
Blue-green algae
Bread mold
Ciliate
Diatom
Earthworm
Fern
Horse
Jellyfish
Lilac bush
Moss
Mushroom
Oak tree
Spider
Spirochete
Yeast

Monera	**Protists**	**Fungi**	**Plants**	**Animals**

COPYRIGHT © 1993 McDONALD PUBLISHING CO.   BIOLOGY

The Roles of Simple Organisms

Many simple organisms affect your life in both beneficial and harmful ways. See how much you know about the roles of microorganisms by taking the following quiz. Write True *or* False *before each statement.*

_____ 1. Viruses are fragments of DNA or RNA that are not alive, but they can reproduce by using the structures within a host cell.

_____ 2. Viruses cause many types of diseases, including colds, flu, and AIDS.

_____ 3. Bacteria do not have a nucleus and are not alive.

_____ 4. Bacteria are not capable of reproduction.

_____ 5. Bacteria play an essential role in the maintenance of life by acting as decomposers and by making nitrogen from the air available to plants.

_____ 6. Bacteria are used to produce vinegar, cheese, yogurt, and many antibiotics.

_____ 7. Bacteria growing on food are always beneficial.

_____ 8. Protists include both one-celled and multi-celled organisms.

_____ 9. Slime molds, algae, and amoebas are protists.

_____ 10. Through photosynthesis, some protists produce their own food.

_____ 11. Fungi are rare organisms.

_____ 12. Fungi, like plants, have chlorophyll.

_____ 13. Fungi include mushrooms, yeasts, and molds and are used to make bread, beer, and many antibiotics.

_____ 14. Fungi, like bacteria, are major decomposers in ecosystems.

_____ 15. All fungi are edible.

Crossword Puzzle on Plants

The crossword puzzle below gives the names of the 10 divisions of plants according to one common classification system. Provide the clues for the puzzle by defining the divisions.

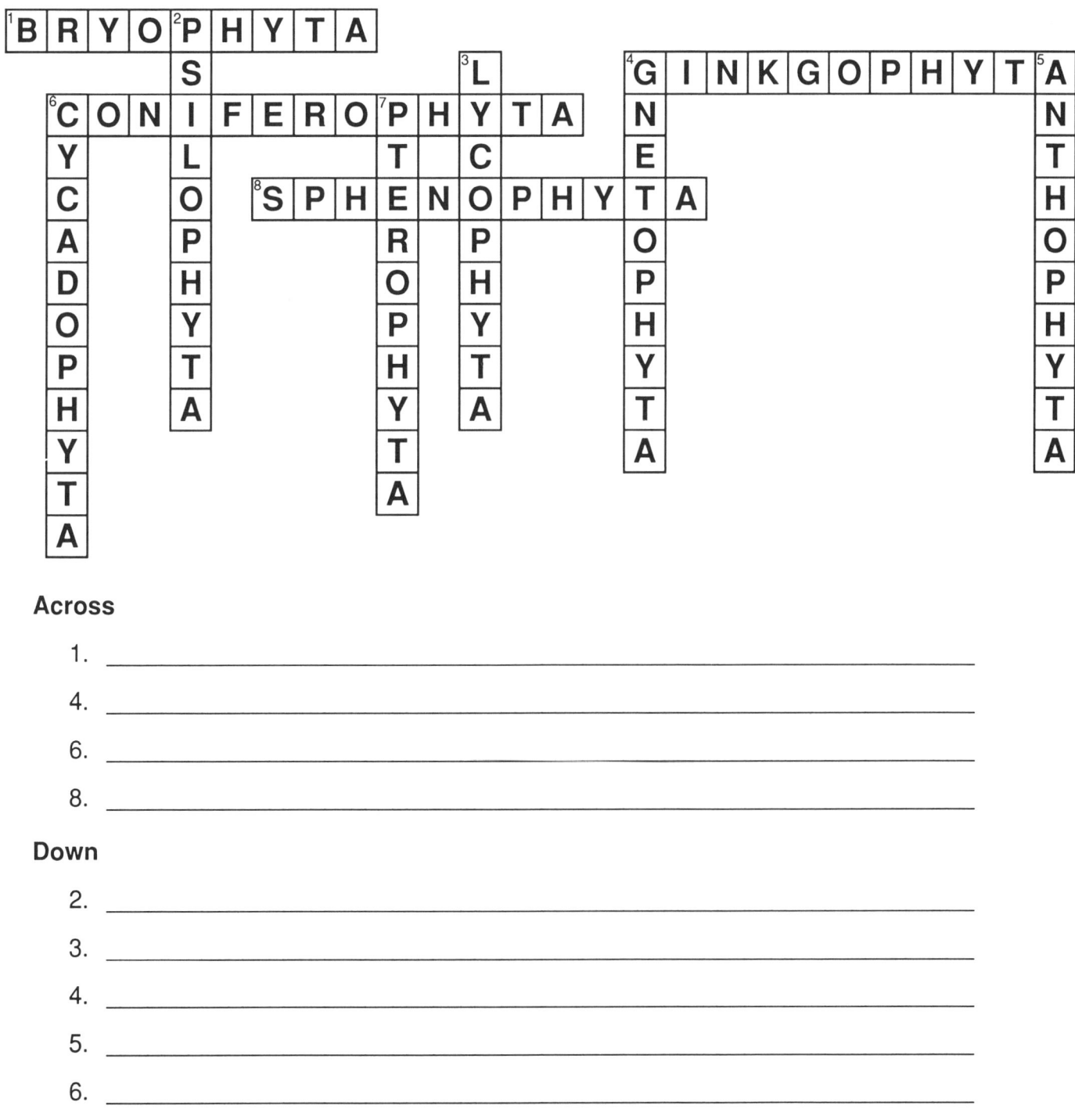

Across

1. _____
4. _____
6. _____
8. _____

Down

2. _____
3. _____
4. _____
5. _____
6. _____
7. _____

Classifying Animals by Phylum

The chart below lists the 10 main phyla of the animal kingdom according to one common classification system. (There are more than 30 phyla in all.) Complete the chart by briefly describing each phylum and by naming a few animals that belong in each group. Be aware that classification systems vary somewhat.

Phylum	Characteristics	Some Animals in the Phylum
1. Chordata		
2. Echinodermata		
3. Mollusca		
4. Chelicerata		
5. Uniramia		
6. Crustacea		
7. Annelida		
8. Platyhelminthes		
9. Cnidaria		
10. Porifera		

Name _____   Vertebrate Classes

Classifying Backboned Animals

The vertebrates, animals with backbones, can be divided into five classes. The chart below summarizes the distinguishing characteristics of these classes. Use the chart to identify each animal listed as fish, amphibian, reptile, bird, or mammal.

Class	Characteristics
Fish	• lives in water • breathes by means of gills
Amphibian	• has scaleless skin • lives part of its life in water and part on land
Reptile	• has dry, scaly skin • breathes by means of lungs
Bird	• has feathers • has wings
Mammal	• feeds its offspring with milk from the mother • has hair, at least at some time in its life

1. Crocodile _____
2. Salamander _____
3. Ostrich _____
4. Rat _____
5. Sea lion _____
6. Snake _____
7. Owl _____
8. Alligator _____
9. Giraffe _____
10. Sea horse _____

11. Duck _____
12. Dolphin _____
13. Frog _____
14. Bat _____
15. Turtle _____
16. Penguin _____
17. Whale _____
18. Lizard _____
19. Shark _____
20. Chicken _____

Name _____   Classifying Plants and Animals by Biomes

Where Plants and Animals Live

The chart below lists seven major biomes and the most important aspect(s) of their climates. Complete the chart by naming a few plants and animals that live in each biome.

Biome	Climate	Types of Plants	Types of Animals
1. Desert	little rain		
2. Grassland	long, cold winter		
3. Savanna	less rainfall than tropical rain forest and seasonal drought		
4. Taiga	long, cold winter; most rainfall in summer		
5. Temperate, deciduous forest	warm summer, cold winter, sufficient rainfall		
6. Tropical rain forest	plentiful rainfall, warm year round		
7. Tundra	cold, dry; permafrost		

Name _____   Ecological Succession

Primary Succession on a Beach Dune

The diagram below shows the stages in plant succession on a sand dune on the central Atlantic coast of the United States. Use the diagram and your own knowledge to answer the questions.

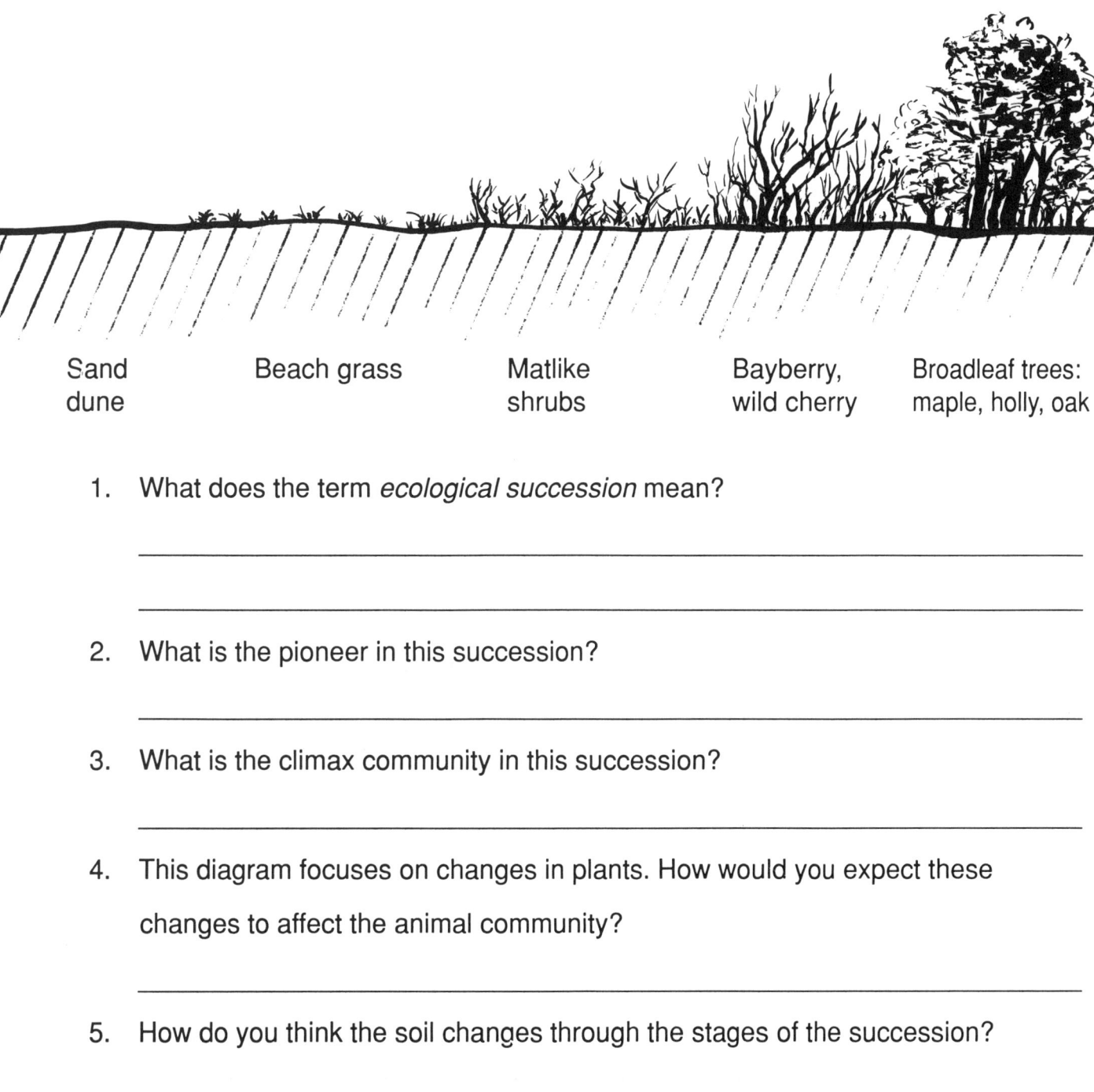

Beach Dune Succession

Sand dune   Beach grass   Matlike shrubs   Bayberry, wild cherry   Broadleaf trees: maple, holly, oak

1. What does the term *ecological succession* mean?

   _____

   _____

2. What is the pioneer in this succession?

   _____

3. What is the climax community in this succession?

   _____

4. This diagram focuses on changes in plants. How would you expect these changes to affect the animal community?

   _____

5. How do you think the soil changes through the stages of the succession?

   _____

People and the Environment

The chart below shows how the human population has grown over the past 200 years. Use the chart to answer the questions.

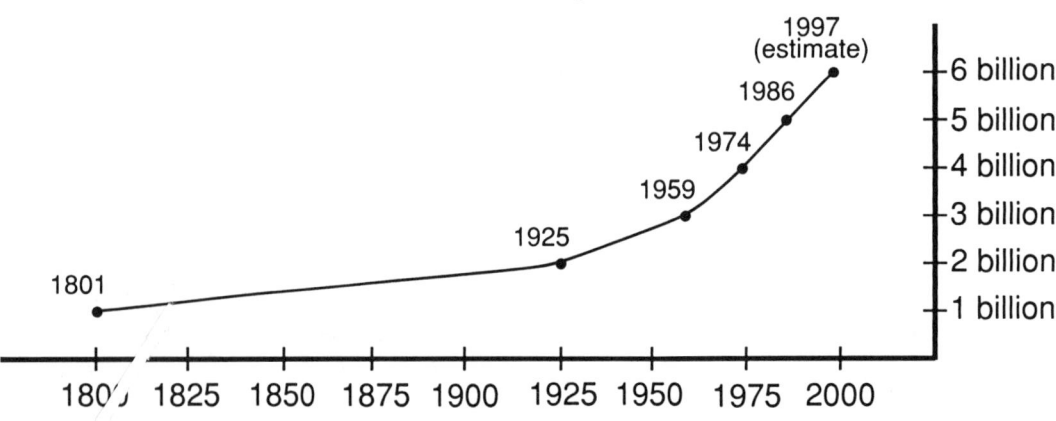

1. How many years did it take for the world population to increase from 1 billion to 2 billion?
   _____

2. How many years did it take for the world population to double from 2 billion to 4 billion?
   _____

3. How many years is it estimated that it will take for the world population to grow from 5 billion to 6 billion?
   _____

4. How many more years did it take for the population to grow from 1 billion to 2 billion than it is estimated it will take for the population to grow from 4 billion to 5 billion? _____

5. Write a statement that summarizes what this graph shows.
   _____

6. Describe the environmental impact that you would expect from this dramatic increase in the human population. Consider the effects on plants, on animals, on human beings, and on ecosystems in general.
   _____
   _____
   _____
   _____

Name _____   Human Respiratory System

The Breath of Life

Label the diagram below using the boldfaced words in the box. Then use the rest of the words to complete the paragraphs about human respiration. Each word will be used only once.

bronchiole
bronchus
capillaries
carbon dioxide
cells
energy
exhaled
lungs
oxygen
trachea

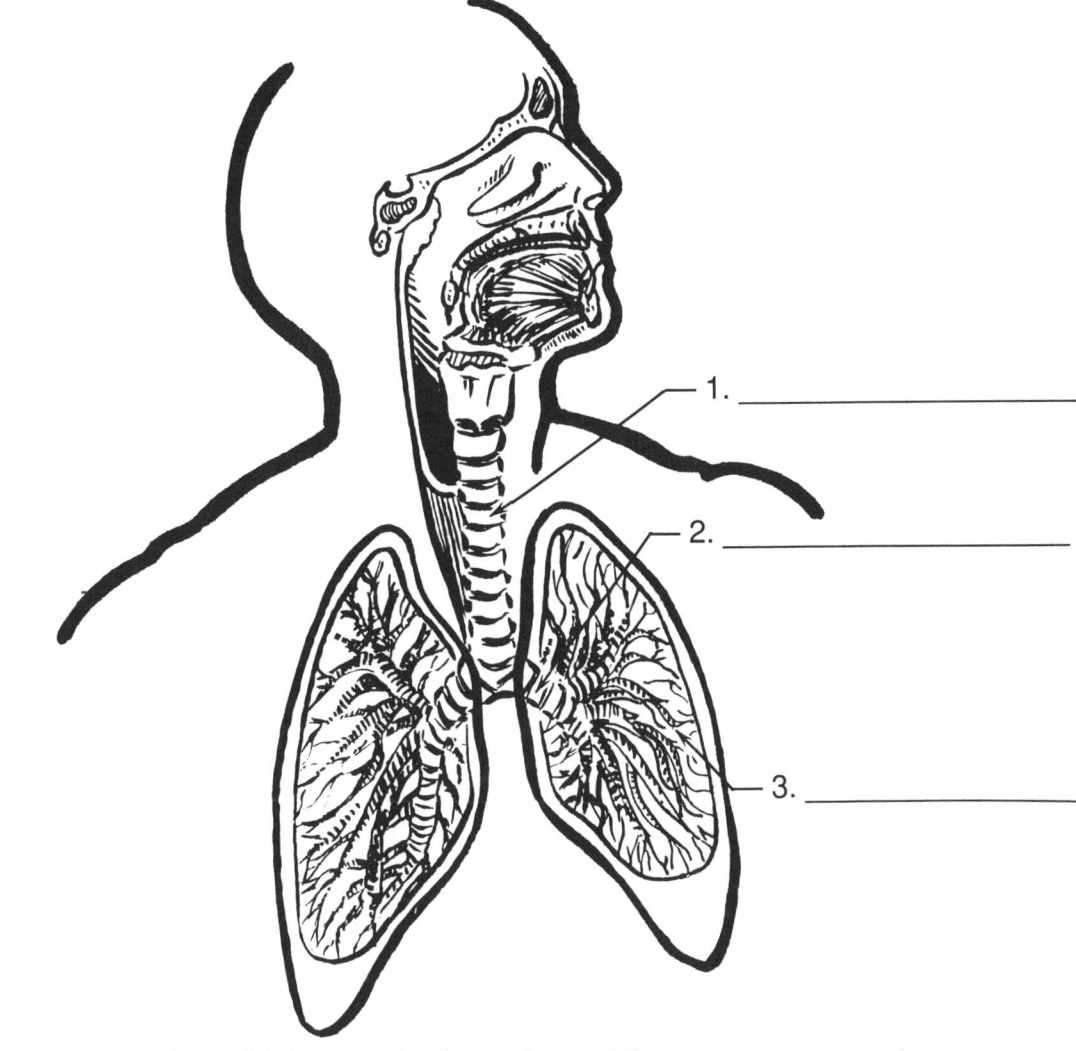

1. _____
2. _____
3. _____

    Respiration is the process by which we take in and use (4) _____ and get rid of (5) _____ . An exchange of these gases occurs in the (6) _____.

    Inside the lungs, oxygen enters blood vessels called (7) _____. The oxygen passes into the blood, which carries it to all the (8) _____ in the body. Within the cells of the body, oxygen is used in chemical reactions to release (9) _____. Meanwhile, in the lungs, carbon dioxide passes out of the blood into the alveoli and is (10) _____.

The Heart Chart

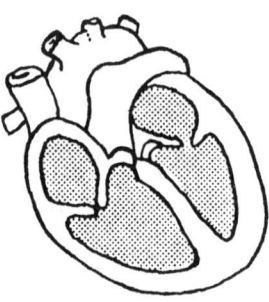

Complete the chart below by briefly describing what each part of the human circulatory system does.

Part of Circulatory System	What It Does
1. Veins	
2. Right atrium and ventricle	
3. Heart valves	
4. Left atrium and ventricle	
5. Arteries	
6. Capillaries	
7. Aorta	
8. Pulmonary artery	
9. Coronary arteries	
10. Pulmonary veins	
11. Superior vena cava	
12. Inferior vena cava	

Name _____   Human Nervous System

Reflex Actions

The knee jerk reflex is a simple reflex that involves the spinal cord but not the brain. The sentences below describe the pathway of a nerve impulse in this reflex, but the sentences are out of order. Write the sentences in order.

- The second impulse reaches the muscle that was stretched, causing the muscle to contract.
- The tap on the tendon stretches the muscle.
- The impulse travels along the axon of a sensory neuron to the spinal cord.
- The whole process is complete and took only a fraction of a second.
- The leg jerks.
- The motor neuron generates a second impulse.
- The receptors produce an impulse.
- The impulse passes through a synapse to a motor neuron.
- The stretched muscle stimulates neurons called receptors.
- A person receives a tap below the kneecap, which hits the tendon there.
- The second impulse is transmitted along the axon of the motor neuron.

1. _____
2. _____
3. _____
4. _____
5. _____
6. _____
7. _____
8. _____
9. _____
10. _____
11. _____

How You Digest Food

The diagram on this page shows the human digestive system. Describe the role of each part of the system in the process of digesting food.

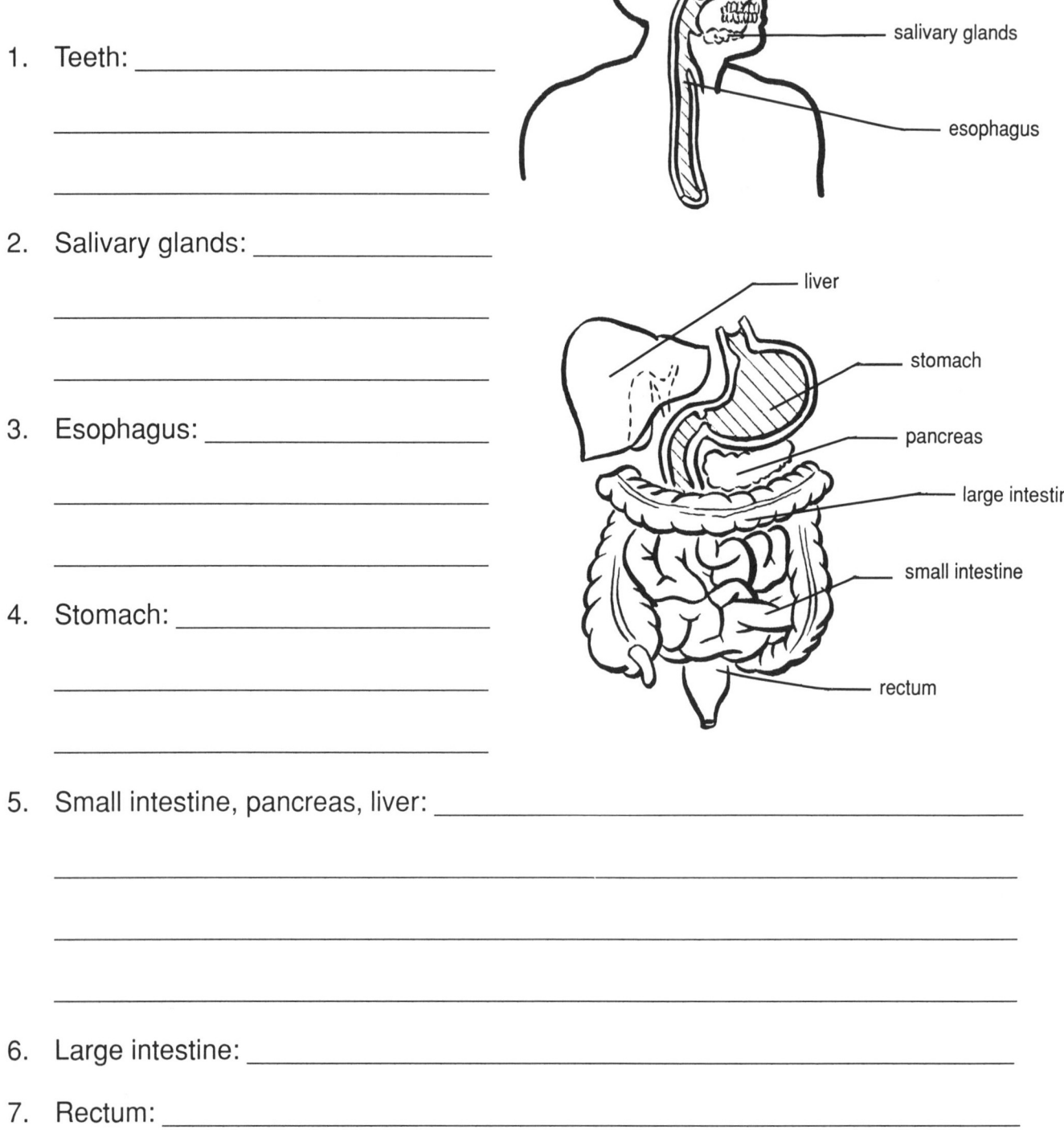

1. Teeth: _____
   _____
   _____

2. Salivary glands: _____
   _____
   _____

3. Esophagus: _____
   _____
   _____

4. Stomach: _____
   _____
   _____

5. Small intestine, pancreas, liver: _____
   _____
   _____
   _____

6. Large intestine: _____

7. Rectum: _____

Planning Nutritious Meals

Use the guidelines below to create a one-week meal plan that is balanced and nourishing. The first day has been done for you.

Recommended Daily Servings from Five Food Groups		
Food Group	**Servings per Day**	**Serving Size**
Bread, cereal, pasta, and other grain products	6-11	1 slice bread or 1 ounce cereal
Fruits	2-4	1 medium-sized apple, orange, banana
Vegetables	3-5	1 cup leafy greens or 1/2 cup other type
Milk and milk products	2-3	1 cup milk or 1 1/2 ounce cheese
Meat, fish, poultry, eggs	2-3	2-3 oz. cooked lean beef or chicken

Meal	Sunday	Monday	Tuesday	Wednesday	Thursday	Friday	Saturday
Breakfast	Toast Orange jc. Cereal Milk						
Lunch	Apple Hamburger on bun Carrot sticks Celery sticks Milk						
Dinner	Veg. salad Chicken Rice Bread Peaches						
Snack	Graham crackers						

Name _____   Human Skeletal System

Crossword Puzzle of the Human Skeleton

Use your knowledge of your body's skeletal system to complete this crossword puzzle.

Across
1. one of the two shoulder bones
3. the shoulder bone that attaches to the sternum
4. one of the two bones of the forearm
5. the bones that form the upper jaw
6. the hip bone
8. one of the two lower leg bones
13. the bones of the hand
14. one of the two bones of the forearm
15. the thigh bone
16. the bones of the head
17. the bones of the chest
18. the finger bones

Down
2. the brain case
3. the wrist bones
7. the chest bone to which the ribs attach
8. the ankle bones
9. the bones that enclose the spinal cord
10. the knee cap
11. the lower jaw bone
12. the upper arm bone
15. one of the two lower leg bones

COPYRIGHT © 1993 McDONALD PUBLISHING CO.   26   BIOLOGY

The Three Kinds of Muscles

A. The statements below describe the functions of the three kinds of muscles in our bodies: skeletal, smooth, and cardiac. Before each statement, write the name of the kind of muscle that performs the function.

_____ 1. Makes our arms, legs, and head move

_____ 2. Moves food through our digestive system

_____ 3. Enables us to stand erect

_____ 4. Pushes blood out of the heart

_____ 5. Makes blood vessels constrict and dilate

_____ 6. Produces a major part of our body heat

_____ 7. Increases and slows the heart rate

_____ 8. Contracts the uterus during childbirth

_____ 9. Contracts the bladder

_____ 10. Enables us to sit and to change our body position

B. Write True or False before each statement below.

_____ 11. Smooth muscles are also called voluntary muscles.

_____ 12. Skeletal muscles pull on the bones and so produce movements.

_____ 13. Smooth muscle fibers have striations and many nuclei.

_____ 14. Most movements involve the action of several muscles.

_____ 15. Cardiac muscle is found only in the heart.

Name _____   Human Immune System

How the Immune System Works

Use the words in the box to complete the description of how the human immune system works. Each word will be used only once.

antibodies	engulfs	phagocytes
antigens	long-term protection	T cells
bacteria	lymphocytes	virus
B cells	macrophages	white blood cells

The immune system consists of (1) _____, which fight bacteria, viruses, and other harmful substances called (2) _____.

There are two main groups of white blood cells: (3) _____ and _____. A phagocyte surrounds and (4) _____ an antigen. The two kinds of lymphocytes, (5) _____ and _____, recognize antigens and inactivate or destroy them.

When an antigen enters the body, the body's immediate response is to send phagocytes called (6) _____ to attack the antigens and to activate T cells. The T cells recognize and destroy body cells infected with a (7) _____. T cells also activate B cells, which are effective against both virus-infected body cells and (8) _____. B cells also produce (9) _____ and thus provide (10) _____ against future infection.

Extension Activity: Immunizations are given to enable a person to develop antibodies to particular diseases. Find out what diseases you have been immunized against.

COPYRIGHT © 1993 McDONALD PUBLISHING CO.   28   BIOLOGY